first animal encyclopedia polar animals

Published 2015 by
A & C Black
an imprint of Bloomsbury Publishing Plc
50 Bedford Square, London, WC1B 3DP
www.bloomsbury.com

Bloomsbury is a registered trademark of Bloomsbury Publishing Plc

ISBN HB: 978-1-4729-1344-9

Produced for Bloomsbury Publishing Plc by Dutch&Dane

A CIP catalogue for this book is available from the British Library.

Picture acknowledgements:
Cover: All Shutterstock.
Insides: All Shutterstock, aside from the following images: p11 top left Doug Perrine/Nature Picture Library;
p21 centre left Doug Allan/Nature Picture Library; p21 bottom right Steven Kazlowski/Nature Picture Library; p24 centre
left Doc White/Nature Picture Library; p25 bottom right Martha Holmes/Nature Picture Library; pp32–33 bottom
Thorsten Milse/Getty Images; p35 bottom Anim1754/NOAA Photo Library; p37 bottom right Roberto Rinaldi/Nature
Picture Library; p38 centre left Uwe Kils/Wikimedia Commons; p38 bottom left NOAA/Monterey Bay Aquarium Research
Institute; p40 centre right Ingo Arndt/Nature Picture Library; p40 bottom left Doug Allan/Nature Picture Library;
p41 top right Visuals Unlimited/Nature Picture Library; p41 bottom right Doug Allan/Nature Picture Library;
p54 bottom left Fred Olivier/Nature Picture Library; pp56–57 centre Christin Khan/NOAA/NEFSC;
p59 top right Glenn Williams/National Institute of Standards and Technology.

This book is produced using paper that is made from wood grown in managed, sustainable forests. It is natural,
renewable and recyclable. The logging and manufacturing process conforms to the environmental regulations
of the country of origin.

Printed in China by Leo Paper Products, Heshan, Guangdong

3 5 7 9 10 8 6 4 2

first
animal
encyclopedia
polar animals

Simon Holland

A & C BLACK
AN IMPRINT OF BLOOMSBURY
LONDON OXFORD NEW YORK NEW DELHI SYDNEY

Contents

Polar worlds

The top and bottom points of planet Earth are the North and South poles, and the areas that surround them are the 'polar' regions. These are the coldest parts of the world, and yet there's life everywhere – both on land and in the seas.

▼ Snowy owls are found all over the Arctic Circle.

North Pole

Equator

South Pole

Earth's axis

▲ The Earth's axis is a straight, invisible line that runs from the North Pole to the South Pole.

The Arctic region

The North Pole is surrounded by the Arctic Ocean and the northern parts of continents that lie within the Arctic Circle. The ocean is partly frozen for most of the year, although some of the ice melts during the summer months.

◄ Walruses are perfectly suited to life in the Arctic region.

A tilted planet

Earth travels around the Sun. Each full circuit lasts a year. As it travels, it is tilted on an angle, which gives each part of the planet its seasons. A region has its summer in the months when it is tilted towards the Sun. Its winter happens when it is tilted away.

▲ As our planet travels around the Sun, it also rotates (spins) around its axis.

Cooler poles

During Earth's year-long circuit, most of the Sun's heat is focused on the middle parts of the planet, around the equator. This is why the Arctic and Antarctic regions are the coolest of all.

The Antarctic region

The South Pole lies on Antarctica, which is surrounded by the Southern Ocean. This continent is covered in a thick sheet of ice, hundreds of metres thick, which spreads into the ocean in all directions.

▶ The Antarctic ice sheet is the biggest mass of frozen water on the planet.

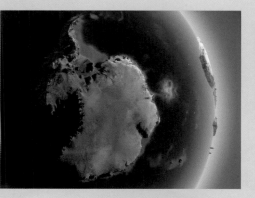

◀ A humpback whale in the Southern Ocean.

▼ Emperor penguins are well adapted to the climate of Antarctica.

AWESOME!

Polar animals have 'adapted' to life in the Arctic or the Antarctic. This means they can survive in extremely dry, cold and harsh weather conditions.

Animals of the poles

The low polar temperatures can make life difficult for some animals. The conditions do not suit animals such as reptiles and amphibians, which rely on warmer or wetter places. However, other animal groups are more able to thrive in the cold.

Mammals

All mammals have a coat of hair or fur, and feed their young on milk produced by the mother. They are warm-blooded, which means their bodies can convert the energy they get from food into vital warmth.

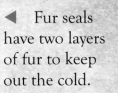

◀ Fur seals have two layers of fur to keep out the cold.

▲ The albatross is a giant bird seen all over the Southern Ocean.

Birds

Birds are feathered creatures adapted for flying. They are warm-blooded, so they can live in both warm and cold places. Many bird species also migrate (travel long distances) to warmer regions when the polar winters get too cold.

▶ Species of cod are found in the waters of the Arctic Circle.

▶ There are at least 24,000 living species of fish, and hundreds of these species live in polar waters.

Fish

Like mammals and birds, fish are 'vertebrates', which means they have a skeleton with a backbone. They have gills, a part of the body that allows them to take oxygen from the water, for breathing. Fish are found in waters all over the planet, including the freezing polar waters.

AWESOME!

The viviparous lizard can live further north than any other reptile. It also gives birth to live young, while most reptiles lay eggs.

▼ The beautiful lion's mane jellyfish lives in the cold, northern waters of the world.

Invertebrates

This animal group covers a huge variety of polar animals, including insects, spiders, jellyfish – and crustaceans such as lobsters, crabs and krill. Echinoderms – such as starfish, sea urchins and sea cucumbers – also live in the Arctic and Antarctic.

Northern waters

The Arctic Circle is dominated by ocean. Many of the animals here either live in the water or depend on the seas for their food. The amount of ice in the sea varies through the year, so some animals have to cope with a constantly changing environment.

Freeze and thaw

At the height of winter, sea ice in the Arctic can cover as much as 16 million square kilometres. During the Arctic's summer months, normally between June and September, more than half of this ice may melt.

▼ Arctic icebergs on the edge of Iceland.

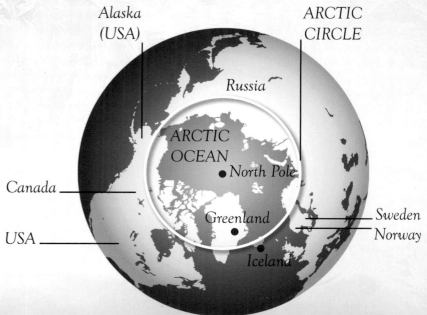

▲ There is no solid land mass beneath the North Pole – only frozen water.

▲ The Greenland shark is also known as the grey shark or gurry shark.

Under the ice

Many animals thrive under the ice. The Greenland shark can survive at depths of up to 600 metres. It usually feeds on other fish, but has also been known to devour mammals such as seals, sea lions – and even polar bears! At more than seven metres long, it is one of the biggest of all sharks.

▶ Polar bears normally hunt seals – but they also feed on dead whales and walruses.

AWESOME!

Beluga whales start to swim south in the autumn. This is to avoid getting trapped under the ice when temperatures drop during the freezing Arctic winter.

Polar hunters

Some animals use the ice as a platform for hunting other animals. Polar bears hang around at the edge of the ice – or look for cracks or holes in the ice – where seals and their pups may pop up from the water to breathe the air.

Arctic lands

The lands of the Arctic Circle include the northern parts of Russia, Finland, Sweden, Norway, Iceland, Greenland, Canada and Alaska. Here are some of the beasts that make their homes up there.

Built for the cold

Musk oxen have a double-layered coat to protect them against the icy northern winds. Outer hairs, called guard hairs, lie on top of a shorter coat of hairs underneath. The two layers trap the air, which then warms up next to the body and keeps out the cold.

▼ Shaggy musk oxen live in northern parts of Canada and Greenland.

Northern deer

Reindeer, or caribou, are found all around the Arctic Circle, from northern Asia and Europe to Greenland and North America. Unlike other types of deer, both the males and females have antlers. They shed (lose) their antlers and grow a new set every year.

◄ Reindeer stay safe by living in large herds.

Alaskan bears

In the rivers of Alaska, in the USA, salmon swim upstream to spawn (lay eggs). During this energetic journey they are often ambushed by hungry brown bears – or 'grizzlies' – that spread out along the rivers to do a spot of fishing.

▶ Minke whales are sleek, quick and agile swimmers.

▼ Brown bears grow to between 1.5 and 2.5 metres long.

Inland minkes

Minke whales are also very widespread. They live in all of the world's oceans and are often spotted venturing into inland waters – such as coastal bays and river estuaries.

AWESOME!

Musk oxen live in herds of up to 100. If they are threatened by predators, such as wolves, they form a defensive circle around their young.

The tundra

The regions on the southern borders of the Arctic are known as the tundra. These vast, flat, treeless areas are cold and dry – and the lower parts of the ground are always frozen. The animals of the tundra have special adaptations that help them to survive.

Bright as snow

Snowy owls have bright yellow eyes, which stand out against their pale feathers. They can turn their head most of the way around, so that they can almost look directly behind them. This makes it hard for their prey – of rabbits and small rodents – to escape from their scary glare!

◀ To protect the owl from the extreme cold, a thick layer of feathers covers the whole of its body and feet.

AWESOME!

As its name suggests, the 'snowshoe' hare has very large, furry feet. When there's a lot of snowfall on the tundra, in winter, these big feet help the hare to push itself around on top of the snow.

▶ Ermines search the tundra wetlands for small rabbits and rodents to eat.

A change of clothes

During each year, the rock ptarmigan's covering of feathers will appear in four different colours. This allows it to blend in with the changing colours of the landscape, through the seasons. This makes it harder for predators to spot the bird.

◀ In winter, this bird sheds its brown plumage to reveal a pure white covering.

Life in the wet

In the summer, when the snow melts, many bogs and marshes form in the tundra. This is because the frozen soil, underground, won't allow the water to drain away. But this is good news for the ermine, a type of weasel that likes to live near wet meadows, marshes, ditches and riverbanks.

Arctic adaptations

Over time, creatures change to become more suited to the natural environment around them. This process is called adaptation. The animals of the polar regions have 'adapted' to cope with the extremely cold and dry conditions.

Cosy coat

The Arctic fox can survive in temperatures as chilly as –50°C. Its white winter coat hides it against its snowy surroundings. In the summer, this coat changes to a brown or grey colour, to disguise the animal among the rocks and plants that emerge once the snow has melted.

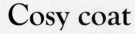
◀ This type of fox has short ears, a small head, a bushy tail and fur-lined feet.

Body warmth

An Arctic hare can hold on to lots of body heat because only very small amounts of its skin are exposed to the air. Groups of these hares sometimes gather together in shelters, dug in the snow, to share their body warmth.

▶ Arctic hares have small ears, and they are completely covered in warm, fluffy fur.

Blubbery bodies

Most of the polar mammals that live in the sea have a thick, fatty layer under their skin. It is called blubber. The fat stored in this layer provides some energy for the animals. The blubber also helps them to float and provides 'insulation' for the body, which means it keeps the heat in and the cold out.

▲ In some sea-going mammals, such as this walrus, blubber makes up almost half the weight of their body.

AWESOME!

The thick-billed murre is a bird that actually swims a lot better than it flies. It likes to eat fish, squid and crustaceans, so it dives through the water – as deep down as 100 metres – to catch its food.

▼ During hibernation, the squirrel's body shivers and shakes once every few weeks to keep it warm enough to survive.

Hibernation

Each year, Arctic ground squirrels spend seven or eight months in hibernation inside their burrows in the ground. This means they go into a state of deep sleep that allows them to escape from the winter chill outside.

Polar bears

The polar bear is beautifully adapted to life in the Arctic. As a warm-blooded mammal, it can convert the energy in its food into warmth – and, like other polar animals, this bear has developed ways of holding on to heat.

Stocky bodies

Adult polar bears are up to two-and-a-half metres long from head to tail. They have a layer of fat, under their skin, which surrounds the body and keeps it warm. On top of this is a thick, warming 'undercoat' of fur.

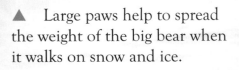
▲ Large paws help to spread the weight of the big bear when it walks on snow and ice.

Colourless coat

On top of the furry undercoat, polar bears have an outer layer of 'guard hairs'. These hairs appear to be white, but actually they have no colour at all. Each one has a hollow centre, which reflects and scatters all the colours in sunlight. This is why the top coat appears to be white.

▲ Underneath its fur, a polar bear's skin is actually black!

Paddle paws

These bears are well built for swimming. Their front paws are very broad and slightly webbed – a little bit like a water bird's feet. The paws act like large paddles, allowing a polar bear to pull itself through the water.

▼ Fur on the bottom of the paws helps the bear to keep a grip on the ice.

AWESOME!

For the first two years of their life, the cubs stay close to their mother. They follow her around and learn how to hunt for food on the ice.

Having cubs

Once they have mated with a male, in springtime, a female polar bear may become pregnant. In the autumn, she will then dig a den in deep drifts of snow. This den will provide warmth and shelter while the bear waits, through the winter, to give birth to her babies.

▶ The mother usually spends two or more months in her den before having her babies.

◀ Female polar bears normally give birth to twin cubs.

19

Seals and sea lions

These meat-eating mammals spend most of their time in the water. Most of them stay near to the coast, however, so that they can come ashore or onto the ice when they need to find a mate and have their babies.

Northern lions

Steller sea lions are the largest and most northern of all sea lion species. They live in the northern Pacific Ocean, along the coastlines of North America and eastern Asia, where they hunt for fish, octopuses, squid and – occasionally – smaller seals.

▼ When fully grown, these sea lions can reach 2.8 metres in length and more than a tonne (1,000 kilograms) in weight.

Fluffy pups

At the end of the mating season, female harp seals gather together on the ice to give birth. When their pups are born, they have extremely fluffy, snow-white fur. As they grow up, their skin loses this fluffiness and turns a light yellow or grey.

AWESOME!

Male hooded seals have a pink-coloured sac inside a hole at the top of their head. They can inflate this sac, like a balloon, to scare off predators or rivals and to attract a female mate.

▲ Harp seal pups are among the most beautiful animals in the Arctic.

▼ Seals are very graceful swimmers, but they sometimes look a bit clumsy on the ice!

Clever tricks

Ringed seals are the smallest and most common species of seals. Polar bears love to eat them. Before climbing onto the ice, the seals blow bubbles in the water and wait to see if a bear sticks its paws or face in. If not, they know they are safe.

Way of the walrus

Walruses are one of the world's most familiar animals. With their tubby bellies, loud barks and large white tusks, they have tonnes of personality – as well as tonnes of weight!

▶ Walrus tusks can be as long as one metre.

▶ Adult male walruses can weigh as much as 1.5 tonnes (1,500 kilograms) or more!

Tubby tummies

Walruses are not as sleek and swift as seals. They have a wide, rounded body covered in thick skin. Beneath the skin lies lots of blubber, which is handy for warmth and also for protection – mainly from the sharp tusks of rival walruses.

AWESOME!

Walruses have very sensitive whiskers, which they use to find their food. They can also spit jets of water to expose hidden creatures on the cloudy sea floor.

Wobbling waddlers

These animals don't chase after fish, so they don't need to be as quick as seals. They gather their food of clams, mussels and other molluscs from the murky seabed. On land they are even slower, pulling their big bodies along with their front flippers.

▲ Walruses sometimes use their tusks to pull themselves up onto land.

Rookeries

When animals have their babies, their main challenge is finding a way to protect the newborns. Walruses gather in very large numbers along coastlines when they are breeding. These areas, known as rookeries, are hard for predators to attack without being seen.

▼ In the social groups, the most important walruses have the longest tusks.

Protecting walruses

Walruses are now a protected species in North America. It is against the law to hunt the animals for their tusks, natural oils, skin and meat. Only the native people of North America are allowed to hunt them, as the animals are a vital source of food.

▲ Walruses are sometimes hunted for their tusks, natural oils, skin and meat.

Whales of the north

Including dolphins and porpoises, there are about 17 different species of whales in the Arctic. There are two main types – toothed whales and baleen whales. Baleens have brush-like plates in their mouths, instead of teeth.

▲ Male narwhals fight each other with their tusks to find out which one is the strongest in their group.

Unicorns of the sea

At first glance, this animal looks like a mythical creature – but it is in fact a pale-coloured porpoise that lives in the rivers and coastal waters of the Arctic. In the males, one of the longer teeth grows into a long, pointed tusk – up to 2.7 metres long.

AWESOME!

When baleen whales feed, they take huge gulps of water. Then they close their mouth and use an enormous tongue to push the water out through their bristly baleen plates. Their meal of fish and small crustaceans gets trapped inside.

◀ The baleen plates hang from the whale's top jaw.

Breaching

Sea mammals – and also some rays and sharks – can 'breach' by launching out of the water and crashing down on the surface. No one knows exactly why they do this. It could be for communication, for cleaning the skin – or just for fun!

▼ Scientists are still trying to work out why whales breach.

▼ Belugas are toothed whales with beautifully pale skin.

Social belugas

Beluga whales are closely related to narwhals, and have a similar body shape. They live together in small social groups, called pods, and communicate with each other using a variety of sounds – such as clicks, clangs and whistles.

Big bowheads

The bowhead is a big beast! It can grow to about 18 or 20 metres long. It is one of three species of 'right whales', which are the second largest animals on the planet – after the enormous blue whale, which can reach 32 metres in length.

▲ The bowhead is named after its three-metre-wide mouth, which is shaped like an archer's bow.

Feeding on fish

There are about 15,000 species of fish in the saltwater seas of the world. Only about 240 of those species live in the northern waters of the Arctic – but they exist in enough numbers to feed a wide range of other animals!

Arctic fish

The fish of the Arctic seas include different types of cod, herring, mackerel, salmon, sand eels, gunnels, greenlings, flatfish, rays, skates, sharks – and many, many more.

▲ A shoal of mackerels swimming in Arctic waters.

▶ During their 120-day feeding season, humpback whales eat up to 2,500 kilograms of food every day.

A small fishing village on the coast of Norway, in northern Europe.

Big feeders

You've already seen how baleen whales remove their food from the water, but what exactly do they eat? Baleens, like the humpback whale, feed on tiny crustaceans (krill, for example), plankton, and small fish such as herrings and mackerels.

Careful fishing

Commercial fishing (catching fish to sell) is very carefully controlled in the Arctic, and is banned in some areas. This is partly to protect the numbers of fish from being reduced too much, and partly to protect the natural environment in the Arctic.

AWESOME!

Now and again, an Arctic tern will swoop down and try to catch a fish as it swims close to the surface of the water. The tern may even try to surprise other birds into dropping their catch!

27

Arctic food chains

All natural habitats have 'food chains', with tiny creatures at the bottom of the chains and large, meat-eating predators at the top. These different food chains usually connect up into more complicated 'food webs'.

Chains of energy

Tiny plants and animals are eaten by larger animals, and then even bigger animals – the 'top predators' – feed on the plant-eating animals. Each creature eats a lot of the food they prey upon. In this way, enough food energy is passed up the chain, from the smallest organisms to the largest predators.

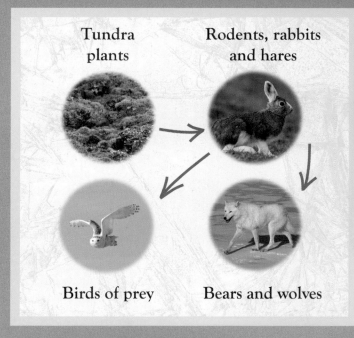

Tundra plants

Rodents, rabbits and hares

Birds of prey

Bears and wolves

▲ A simple food chain from the Arctic tundra.

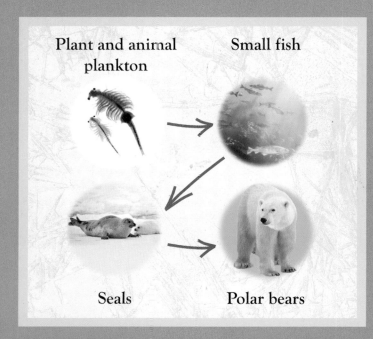

Plant and animal plankton

Small fish

Seals

Polar bears

▲ A simple food chain from the Arctic seas.

Primary producers

Plants on land, and the tiny bits of plant and animal plankton in the water, are a food chain's 'primary producers'. They create the energy that is consumed by small animals such as rabbits, rodents, small fish, crustaceans, jellyfish and squid.

The Arctic gyrfalcon mainly eats other birds – but it also preys on small mammals such as rodents, rabbits and hares.

Top predators

The top predators of a certain habitat, or ecosystem, are normally the larger meat-eaters. In the Arctic, for example, the biggest hunters include polar bears, Arctic wolves, seals, and birds of prey such as owls, hawks and falcons.

AWESOME!

The blue whale is the largest animal of all time. At certain times of the year, it eats more than three tonnes of krill every day – to keep its massive body going.

The Arctic wolf mainly feeds on musk oxen, Arctic hares and caribou (reindeer).

In winter, Arctic hares dig through the snow to find plants to eat.

Northern birds

The birds of the Arctic are very adaptable. They can stay in northern regions to feed while the weather suits them, and migrate to more southern areas if the winter temperatures get too chilly. Some of them spend a lot of their life at sea.

Mass migration

Snow geese spend the colder months in the south. When the Arctic winter ends, they head north – towards the tundra regions – in huge numbers. When the sky fills with snow geese, it is often called a 'snowstorm'.

AWESOME!

You can recognise a northern fulmar bird by its peculiar noises. While eating, it sounds like it's chuckling at something funny. While breeding, fulmars grunt loudly at each other.

A migrating flock
of Canada geese.

Puffin power

Atlantic puffins are dedicated
seabirds. They spend almost all
of their time on the water, either
resting on the surface or swimming
underwater. They use their wings
to pull themselves through the
water, while their webbed feet act
like rudders to help them steer.

Flying in formation

Canada geese also fly south if
the temperatures in the north
get too cool in winter. When
they decide to migrate, they
fly in their famous V-shaped
formations, honking loudly as
they go. They mainly use the
same routes, with familiar
'rest stops' along the way.

Snow geese fly in
U-shaped formations.

Puffins can dive up to 60
metres, or more, underwater.

Raising young

Breeding in the wild is always a challenge for polar animals. The parents need to find a safe place to nest or give birth, so that their babies will have the best chance of survival when they come into the world.

Calving

When whales have their babies, it is called calving. Beluga whales don't leave the Arctic region to breed, but they do head to coastal bays and river estuaries where the water is warmer. The females normally give birth to just one baby, called a calf, every three years.

▲ As soon as it is born, a beluga calf is able to swim alongside its mother.

▶ Even if there are lots of young seals around, a mother can usually recognise the smell of her own pups.

▶ Ringed seal pups are born with a coat of white fur, which they lose after two or three weeks.

Clifftop nesting

Like many seabirds, kittiwakes spend most of their time out at sea when they are not breeding. But when it is time to have their babies, they build nests on very small 'shelves', high up on the side of cliffs.

▲ These high nests look dangerous, but they allow the parents to raise their chicks without other birds getting in the way.

Snow caves

Female ringed seals build a 'birth lair' – just like some other mammals do – when they are ready to give birth. They dig under drifts of snow to create the nest, which will protect both the mother and pup from the extreme weather, as well as from predators.

AWESOME!

When northern gannets breed, they get together in huge 'bird cities' on the cliffs of remote, offshore rocks and islands. Some colonies have been used by the birds for hundreds of years.

▶ These nesting sites are crowded, and very noisy!

North to south

When animals travel long distances for a certain purpose, it is called migration. Animals migrate if they need to have their babies in warmer places, or if they need to find more food at certain times of the year.

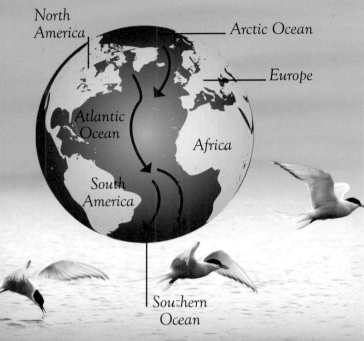

▲ Arctic terns travel at least 35,000 kilometres every year.

Turn of the tern

The Arctic tern is a small bird, but its migration route is the longest of any animal. It spends its summer in the Arctic Circle, where it nests, and heads south when it feels the temperatures dropping. It then heads to the opposite end of the world, where it will be summer.

Feeding and breeding

The summer feeding grounds for grey whales are found between Alaska and northeastern Siberia. These waters are too chilly for breeding, so every year the whales head south – all the way to the waters off Baja California, in Mexico – to have their babies.

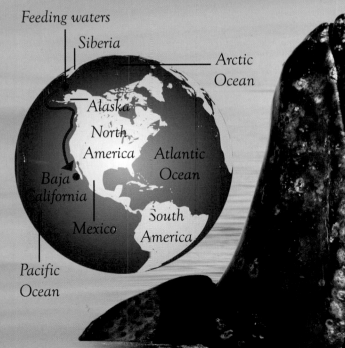

◄ Every year, grey whales travel at least 20,000 kilometres to Mexico and back.

Global humpbacks

Humpback whales are found in all the oceans of the world, but they all behave in a similar way when it's time for them to breed. They feed in waters closer to the poles, and then travel long distances to breeding areas in warmer waters, much closer to the equator.

▼ A blue whale calf.

▲ Humpback whales have breeding grounds in the Pacific, Atlantic and Indian oceans.

AWESOME!

Blue whale calves are the biggest babies in the world. When they are born, they are already about eight metres long and weigh about two-and-a-half tonnes.

Bottom of the world

Unlike the North Pole, the South Pole is on a continent – Antarctica. It is not a natural home for humans, although many scientists visit Antarctica, or stay at research stations, to study the environment and the wildlife.

South America

Pacific Ocean

Atlantic Ocean

Southern Ocean

South Pole

Antarctica

Australia

South Africa

▲ Antarctica only gets 200 millimetres of rain every year, along its coasts – and even less rainfall inland.

A polar desert

When we think of a desert, we normally imagine somewhere hot and dry. However, the chilly continent of Antarctica is also a desert, because it receives very little rainfall. In fact, it is the biggest desert in the world.

▼ Huge chunks of ice break away from the Antarctic ice sheet and become icebergs.

Southern mammals

Just like in the Arctic, there is a wide range of mammals living in the Southern Ocean. These include toothed whales, baleen whales and seals.

▲ This minke whale is coming to the surface to breathe.

► An Antarctic midge.

Southern invertebrates

As well as mammals, birds and fish, the Antarctic is also home to some incredible 'echinoderms' – the group of animals that includes starfish, feather stars, sea cucumbers and sea urchins. Some types of coral can also live in these colder waters.

Creatures of the ice

Almost all the animals of the Antarctic live around the edge of the continent's enormous ice sheet, which covers about 14 million square kilometres. Ocean-going creatures, such as seals and penguins, use the surrounding icebergs as places where they can rest – in safety – between feeding visits to the sea.

▼ This echinoderm is a multi-armed 'sun star'.

Icy adaptations

Fresh water freezes at 0°C, but salty seawater freezes at a slightly lower temperature. The fish of the Antarctic have special adaptations that enable them to live in sea temperatures as low as about –2°C.

◄ Many icefish have white or see-through blood!

Antifreeze fish

Icefish are specially adapted to Antarctic conditions. Some of them have a larger, more powerful heart to keep the blood circulating in freezing-cold water. Others have substances in their blood, called glycoproteins, which stop the blood from freezing when the temperature of the water dips below zero.

▼ Rattail fish grow to about 40 centimetres long.

Rats' tails

Some southern fish live at much deeper depths, where they find it easier to get their food. The rattail fish – named after its long, thin tail – is a deep-water scavenger. It can live at depths of up to 5,000 metres, and eats anything it can find, living or dead!

◀ A female gentoo penguin feeding one of her chicks.

Fish for all

In the polar regions, fish are a vital source of food energy for sea mammals and birds such as seals, whales and penguins. Female penguins swallow a belly-full of fish, krill or squid, and then 'regurgitate' (bring up) the food into the mouths of their young.

AWESOME!

Southern minke whales are small baleen whales that love to feed on krill and small fish. They have very bad breath and are sometimes known as 'stinky minkes'!

Big and toothy

Some fish have evolved to have a larger body, so that they can eat as wide a range of food as possible. The Patagonian toothfish has a big mouth with large, spiky teeth. These adaptations allow it to eat both fish and squid. Some toothfish are more than two metres long.

Polar invertebrates

Invertebrates are creatures that don't have a backbone, and they live in almost every environment on the planet. Here are some examples that live in the waters of the Southern Ocean.

▶ Jellyfish have no blood – and no brains!

Antarctic jellies

Jellyfish are beautiful animals, wherever they are found in the world. Some of the species found in the Antarctic are extremely small. This one, from the Weddell Sea, is about two centimetres long.

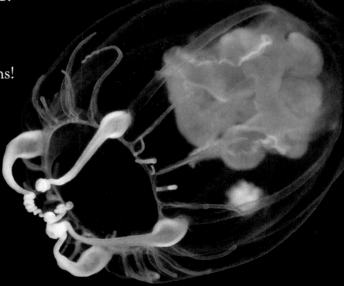

Waste collectors

Sea cucumbers are a type of echinoderm that can live on seabeds all over the world. They were given this name because they have soft bodies and are shaped like cucumbers. The body of a sea cucumber has lots of tiny, tube-like feet, which sweep particles of food into the animal's mouth.

◀ Sea cucumbers eat tiny bits of plants, animals and other bits of seafloor waste.

▶ This sea spider, from the Antarctic waters, is only a few centimetres wide.

AWESOME!

The warty bobtail squid lives in northern and Arctic seas. It's tiny! It's less than five centimetres long – but it can live in very cold water, hundreds of metres below the sea's surface.

Sea spiders

Antarctic sea spiders grow much more slowly than those in warmer parts of the world, but some end up being much, much bigger. Most of them are about the same size as an adult's hand, but those from cooler, deeper waters can grow even larger.

Giant isopods

Large numbers of these alien-like crustaceans live around the coastlines of Antarctica and the islands of the Southern Ocean. They live on the seabed and scavenge around for echinoderms and other types of food.

▶ This isopod lives on the seabed, as deep down as 550 metres or more.

Mammals of the south

The mammals of Antarctica include seals, toothed whales and baleen whales. Seals belong to a group called 'pinnipeds' – along with sea lions and walruses – while whales belong to the 'cetaceans' group, which also includes dolphins and porpoises.

Ice elephants

Southern elephant seals are the largest seals of all. They weigh a whopping 4,000 kilograms – and some of the males are more than six metres long. Their bodies can hold on to a lot of oxygen, which means they can make deep dives – down to about 1,600 metres underwater.

◄ Battles between the male elephant seals often end with lots of loud bellowing!

▶ Weddell seals can swim down to 600 metres underwater, or even deeper, in search of their food.

Southern-most seals

Weddell seals are big and fat, weighing as much as 500 kilograms. They probably live further south than any other mammal. They feed on icefish and Antarctic cod, and find plenty of them deep under the ice.

◀ This massive seal feeds on squid and fish, often in very deep water.

Crab- or krill-eaters?

Funnily enough, crabeater seals don't actually eat crabs. The name 'crabeater' describes their teeth, which are perfectly designed for gathering up small crustaceans to eat – but the crustaceans they prefer to munch are krill, not crabs.

▼ Crabeater seals swim under the ice to find lots of krill to eat.

Feeding habits

Krill are small, shrimp-like crustaceans, but they exist in the Southern Ocean in their millions. They are a vital part of the food chain in Antarctica, where fish, birds and mammals all feed on them.

The krill chain

Krill feed on tiny plant plankton, which floats in the water or grows on the underside of the sea ice. When fish, birds and mammals eat large numbers of krill, the food energy goes up the food chain – up to the largest predators, which feed on the fish, birds and smaller mammals.

▼ At certain times of the year, there may be more than five million tonnes of krill in the waters around Antarctica.

▼ Each krill is just five or six centimetres long.

Bubble nets

Humpback whales have been spotted blowing 'bubble nets'. They release bubbles of air through the blowhole on the top of their body – and the bubbles trap their prey of krill and small fish. Then they take it in turns to gobble up the food.

▲ Humpbacks swim through their 'bubble nets' to feed on the prey they have trapped.

◄ Food gets caught in the baleen plates as water is squeezed out of the throat and mouth.

Rorqual whales

Rorquals – such as blue, fin, sei and humpback whales – feed by taking in huge mouthfuls of water, which are full of food. Their throat is designed to expand like a balloon as the water pours in. They have a massive tongue to help push all the water out, through the baleen plates, as their jaws close.

Skim feeders

In the summer months, right whales spend up to six months feeding in waters where their food is most plentiful. They swim through swarms of plankton, krill (and other small crustaceans) with their mouth open. When they do this at the water's surface, it is known as 'skim feeding'.

AWESOME!

During its feeding season, a blue whale will eat constantly for about 120 days. On each day it will consume at least 3,500 kilograms, or three-and-a-half tonnes, of krill.

45

Southern hunters

Southern waters are patrolled by two of the world's most powerful predators – the orca and the leopard seal. Leopard seals live only in the Antarctic, while orcas are also found towards the equator and in the Arctic.

The killer whale

Orcas, otherwise known as killer whales, are the largest animals in the dolphin family. Adults are between seven and ten metres long, with sharp teeth that are up to ten centimetres long.

▼ An orca breaching, or 'cresting'.

▼ If there are not many seals around, orcas will sometimes chase after penguins.

Splash and grab

Seals are the favourite food of these magnificent animals, although they also feed on fish, seabirds, squid and sometimes penguins. They wait around for seals and penguins to enter the water, or just grab them from the shore or a shelf of ice.

Sea leopards

These sleek, dangerous animals are named after leopards, because of the black spots that decorate their light grey coat. They have a very long, slender and flexible body, which can move through the water with speed.

▲ Leopard seals are up to three-and-a-half metres long.

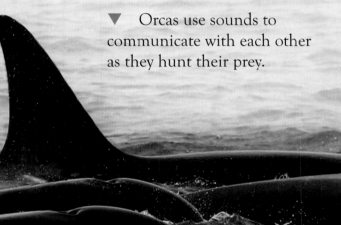

▼ Orcas use sounds to communicate with each other as they hunt their prey.

AWESOME!

The leopard seal has a large head and an impressive set of sharp teeth. The pointed teeth at the front of the jaws are designed to sink into their prey, so that the victims can't get away.

▲ Orcas hunt in groups, or pods, of up to 40 animals.

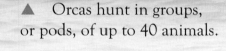

Food on the shelf

Their powerful jaws and long teeth allow leopard seals to eat other seals, as well as fish, shellfish, squid and penguins. Like orcas, they often wait by or underneath shelves of ice, so they can grab penguins as soon as they jump into the water.

◀ These seals also snatch seabirds as they rest on the surface of the sea.

47

Antarctic studies

No place on this planet is as cold, dry and windy as the continent of Antarctica. Scientists are always studying the animals that live in this extreme environment, to learn more about their amazing abilities.

Animal diaries

Wildlife experts and biologists study the lives of polar animals in detail. Some follow every single moment of any animal's daily routine, to build up a 'diary' of how it moves, feeds, protects itself or has its babies.

▶ Weather balloons are used to carry scientific instruments up into the atmosphere.

Weather watching

The way an animal behaves is often controlled by the weather. Scientists study the climate and weather conditions in places like the Antarctic, to see how environmental changes affect the way animals live.

▲ Weather and climate experts study icebergs to learn more about how the Antarctic ice shelf breaks up during the year.

An Antarctic research station.

Saving energy

Living in the polar regions is tough, so animals need to find ways to save energy, keep warm, and protect themselves during difficult seasons such as the Arctic or Antarctic winter. Scientists spend a lot of time studying these habits.

▼ Animals use body heat to keep their babies warm and healthy.

Human pressures

Scientists and conservationists keep an eye on human activities such as fishing, hunting or drilling for oil and other natural resources. These activities sometimes destroy or put pressure on the natural homes of polar animals.

▼ This oil pipeline runs through the northern state of Alaska in the USA.

Southern birds

All over the world, birds need to find the best ways to find their food, cope with the changing temperatures and have their babies. Here are some birds who have adapted very well to life in the deep south.

A mate for life

It can take a wandering albatross years to find a mate to have babies with – but once a male and a female have paired up, they stay together for life. When they first get together, the birds spend time displaying their wings to each other and preening each other.

▼ This mating display helps the two birds to get to know each other.

▶ Snow petrels make their nests in deep openings in rocks or cliffs.

Antarctic eggs

The snow petrel is one of only a few birds that lay their eggs in the Antarctic region – and nowhere else. This species of bird lives and feeds almost entirely in Antarctic waters, and has been spotted as far south as the South Pole itself!

AWESOME!

Wilson's storm petrels are found in all the seas of the southern hemisphere (south of the equator). They also travel to seas north of the equator.

Big bullies

The south polar skua is a big bird, at least half a metre long. It normally feeds on fish and krill, but also eats penguin eggs and chicks.

▲ This bird nests and lays its eggs on the Antarctic continent.

Penguin patrol

There are 17 different species of penguins in the world today, and all of them live south of the equator. The penguins of Antarctica include the Adélie, emperor, chinstrap and gentoo penguins.

Life in black and white

You can recognise a chinstrap penguin by the thin, dark line that runs across its cheeks and under its chin. They have a pure white face and belly, and can grow to almost 70 centimetres tall.

▼ Penguin feathers are short and thick. They are designed for keeping out the cold – not for flying.

AWESOME!

Macaroni penguins have an amazing golden crest, which grows on their forehead and sweeps back above their eyes – like a funky hairstyle!

▲ Adélie penguins live on the continent of Antarctica, and on the islands that surround it.

Adélie exercises

Adélie penguins are not lazy. During their daily hunt for food (of fish, krill and squid) they will swim as many as 300 kilometres. In winter and early spring, when there is more sea ice around Antarctica, they have to walk about 50 kilometres just to reach the water.

Water wings

Penguins are well adapted for life in the sea. Over time, their wings have evolved (developed) into flippers for swimming. Their small, sleek bodies allow them to slip through the water with ease.

▶ Gentoo penguins have bright red-orange beaks and a 'cap' of pure white feathers.

Penguin families

Emperor penguins are the tallest and heaviest of all penguins. They live and breed on the Antarctic ice, and have to cope with some of the roughest weather on the planet.

▼ A male keeps an egg warm in his 'brood pouch'.

An emperor's eggs

Once a female emperor penguin has laid an egg, it's up to the male to look after it and keep it warm. The males keep the eggs in a warm space between their feet and a soft, feathery pouch of skin above.

Huddling

Emperors breed further south than any other penguin species, even during the harsh Antarctic winter, when temperatures can plummet to as low as –60°C. While they are warming the eggs, the males huddle together in large groups.

Female hunters

While the males care for the eggs, the females go hunting for food. Sometimes, they will need to travel as far as 80 kilometres to reach the sea. They will then eat as many krill, fish and squid as they possibly can.

▲ Emperor penguins can dive deeper than 550 metres in search of food.

▲ This chick is covered in a warm, fluffy coat of grey 'down' feathers.

▼ The male emperors take it in turns to stand in the middle of the group, where it is warmest.

Feeding the chicks

When a female returns with a belly full of food, she 'regurgitates' it. This means she brings it up into her mouth again, so that she can pass it into the mouth of her newly-hatched chick. Meanwhile, the males go off to the ocean to feed.

AWESOME!

Adult emperor penguins can reach about 115 centimetres in height. That's taller than a lot of six-year-old children!

Whales of the south

Whales live in all the oceans of the world, from the north to the south. Every toothed and baleen whale species has its own unique set of habits, which animal experts are still finding out about.

Blowholes

Whales and dolphins breathe air, just like we do. This is why they have to come to the surface from time to time. They have either one or two 'blowholes' on the top of their bodies, a bit like our nostrils, which allow them to take in air.

▼ When a whale breathes out, a big spray of water and air – called a spout – is often thrown out of the blowhole.

▲ Sei whales enjoy swimming in deep waters, further from the shore.

Sperm whales

Sperm whales are the biggest of all the toothed whales. They can reach 18 metres in length and 40 tonnes in weight. They appear in all the oceans of the world, including polar seas in both the north and the south.

▲ Up to 20 sperm whales live together in groups, or pods.

◄ Sperm whales search the depths for their favourite food – giant squid.

Deep feeders

Sperm whales are one of the deepest-diving animals in the world. They can hold their breath for about an hour, and spend most of their time at depths of 1,000 metres or more. On some dives, they may even go deeper than 3,000 metres.

AWESOME!

Humpback whales sing to each other, across great distances, for many hours. The songs may be used to attract a mate.

Sei, you're speedy!

Sei whales live in all the oceans, and are among the fastest whales. They can travel at speeds of up to 50 kilometres per hour. The sei is one of the largest of the rorqual whales, after the blue whale and the fin whale.

Arctic pressures

The polar regions are very sensitive habitats. They are easily affected by human activities, gradual changes in the weather and climate – and especially by the process of global warming.

▼ Temperatures in the Arctic are rising two or three times faster than anywhere else.

Global warming

Global warming is the gradual increase in the temperature of our planet's atmosphere. It is caused by certain waste gases that are being released into the atmosphere, which trap more of the Sun's heat.

▼ Melting sea ice allows commercial ships to sail through the Arctic Ocean.

Warming seas

The rising temperatures in the atmosphere cause the seas to get warmer. This means that more of the ice is melting in the polar regions at certain times of the year. Without the ice, many polar animals will have nowhere to find their food or have their babies.

Noise pollution

There is a lot of natural oil and gas in the Arctic, which means lots of commercial ships pass through. The noises they create can confuse animals in the northern seas, such as narwhals, preventing them from communicating to find food, find a mate and protect their young.

▲ Narwhals have been hunted for their tusks for centuries.

NOT SO AWESOME!

Animals such as the Arctic fox find life tough if their usual food – of small rodents, hares, birds and fish – is in short supply.

Hunting

Because they have such beautiful, valuable fur, harp seal pups have been hunted for more than two hundred years. These seals, too, are at risk from the melting of the sea ice, which is their natural habitat. Many are also killed by boats and oil spills.

▲ Hundreds of thousands of harp seals are killed by humans every year.

Antarctic troubles

The Antarctic region is also threatened by global warming and rising sea temperatures. Like the Arctic, it also faces pressure from human activities such as shipping and tourism.

Losing the krill

Scientists believe that the numbers of krill in the ocean have dropped by about 80 per cent over the last 40 or 50 years. This may be due to the loss of sea ice, through global warming, which is where the krill find the algae that they feed on.

AWESOME!

Scientists studying whales can tell each of them apart because of the markings on their tail fins, or flukes. Each tail is different – just like human fingerprints!

▼ Without krill, most animals in the Antarctic would struggle to survive.

▶ Tourist trips usually take place during the Antarctic summer, from November to March.

▼ The studies of the fur seals on Bird Island, Antarctica, began in 1981.

Increasing tourism

Back in the 1950s, only a few hundred tourists visited Antarctica each year. Nowadays, tens of thousands of people come to the continent. The trips are usually carefully controlled by expert guides, and tourists are reminded that they should never disturb the animals.

Proud survivors

Fur seals are found in both Arctic and Antarctic waters. In the 18th and 19th centuries, they were hunted almost to extinction in the Antarctic. Luckily, a group of fur seals survived on an island called Bird Island. The seals here are now closely monitored by conservationists.

Glossary

Adapted Gradually developed to suit a particular purpose or environment.

Algae Tiny, plant-like living things.

Amphibians Animals, such as frogs, toads and newts, that have smooth, damp skin.

Birds Animals, such as gulls, albatrosses and penguins, that have wings, feathers and beaks.

Breeding Having babies.

Cetaceans Whales, dolphins and porpoises.

Conservation Protecting or looking after an animal, plant or place for the future.

Continent A huge expanse of land on the Earth's surface. Antarctica is a continent.

Coral A hard, shell-like substance made by tiny creatures called coral polyps.

Crustacean An invertebrate animal that lives in the sea. Lobsters, crabs, shrimps and krill are all crustaceans.

Echinoderm A sea-dwelling invertebrate animal, such as a starfish or sea urchin.

Equator The invisible 'central line' that runs around the middle of the Earth.

Estuary The mouth of a large river, where it meets the salty water of the sea.

Evolution Animals 'evolve' (change or adapt) over long periods of time to become better suited to their natural surroundings.

Extinction A species of plant or animal is 'extinct' if it has died out forever.

Fish An animal, such as a cod, ray or shark, that has fins and a sleek, streamlined body. Many species of fish have scaly bodies.

Habitat The place where a species of animal or plant is found and is adapted to living in.

Invertebrate Invertebrate animals do not have bones, or a backbone, although some have a hard outer casing.

Krill Very small, shrimp-like sea creatures that swim in huge shoals, or swarms.

Mammals Animals, such as whales, seals, bears and humans, that have hair or fur covering their bodies and feed their young on milk produced by the mother.

Mating When male and female animals, of the same species, get together to have babies.

Migrate To travel long distances, to find food or to mate and have babies.

Mollusc An invertebrate animal such as a slug, snail or mussel.

Oxygen A gas that animals need to breathe, which is found in both air and water.

Pinnipeds A group of meat-eating sea mammals that includes seals and walruses.

Plankton Tiny plants and animals that drift around in seawater.

Plumage Another word for a bird's feathers, especially if they are long or brightly coloured.

Pollution Anything that harms a natural environment, such as noise or chemical waste.

Porpoise A small, toothed whale with a blunt, rounded snout (nose and mouth).

Predator An animal that hunts and feeds on other animals.

Pregnant A female animal is pregnant when a baby is developing inside her.

Prey An animal that is hunted and eaten by another animal.

Reptiles Animals, such as lizards, turtles and crocodiles, that have dry, scaly skin.

Scavenger An animal that feeds on old, dead animals or bits of food left by other animals.

Spawning Laying eggs.

Species A group of living things that have similar features. Living things of the same species can mate and produce young.

Vertebrate Vertebrate animals have a skeleton with a backbone, or spine.

Warm-blooded Warm-blooded animals can keep their bodies at a temperature that is (often) warmer than their surroundings.

Index

Further Information

BOOKS

First Animal Encyclopedia: Birds
By Mike Unwin
(A & C Black, 2014)

First Animal Encyclopedia: Rainforests
By Anita Ganeri
(A & C Black, 2014)

First Animal Encyclopedia: Seas and Oceans
By Anna Claybourne
(A & C Black, 2014)

First Animal Encyclopedia
By Anita Ganeri
(A & C Black, 2013)

ONLINE RESOURCES

World Wildlife Fund (WWF)
See amazing videos and photographs, and find out how polar animals survive in their natural habitats:
http://www.worldwildlife.org/habitats/polar-regions

EcoKids education and activity pages
Here you'll find lots of games and activities that will teach you all about the people, plants and animals of North America and the Arctic Circle:
http://www.ecokids.ca/pub/eco_info/topics/canadas_north/nature/wildlife.cfm